I0756318

FINISHING LINE PRESS
www.finishinglinepress.com

If There's a Place to Keep it All It's Here

poems by

Jeff King

Finishing Line Press
Georgetown, Kentucky

If There's a Place to Keep it All It's Here

ISBN 979-8-89990-465-3 First Edition

ACKNOWLEDGMENTS

The following poem originally appeared in another place, for which I would like to thank the editors:

Heavy Feather Review, "What the Body Will Say When You're Dead"

Publisher: Leah Huete de Maines
Editor: Christen Kincaid
Cover Art: Adam Findley
Author Photo: Joshua Foo
Cover Design: Elizabeth Maines McCleavy

Order online: www.finishinglinepress.com
also available on amazon.com

Author inquiries and mail orders:
Finishing Line Press
PO Box 1626
Georgetown, Kentucky 40324
USA

Contents

Dedicated to those I've known in life
that I have called a friend

All the Things I've Left on the Ground

At first, there seemed a different beat to pursue.
I stopped dawdling in a flower patch any longer,
exited the grass and branches. The living
they go elsewhere, often not at their choosing,
as a bouquet or boutonniere, in someone's hand
leaving a field. I am sure my life is a collection of messes,
not one dish stacked neatly on a shelf, no containment
in the sock drawers rambling, not even my t-shirts
in one location, each left to find its own way to the laundry.
I've tried to find my life. I never achieved a solid state,
with too many places to look, so many flowers
to leave laying in a field unpicked as though I could choose
just one as a reminder. There is no way to remember
this life, it all falls apart into shreds of dandelions.

Hollywood Darkroom

If we are ever ourselves, who is it looking
back at us when a mirror approaches. Dark
like horsehair and equally coarse, each of us
sees what we want. Some, not all, want perfect
images to comfort their children, a Hollywood
vision, photographs simple with edges older
than their lifetime showing movie stars reassuring
it's going to be ok. There's nothing real in light
cast across photo paper to capture a picture
of people who are only acting like people,
with makeup and clothes too elaborate
for any other reason. Ask: what is light?
How many pictures do you have
that make you believe you can stop motion.

Any Stable Surface

Finer lines in her face, creeping outward from a smile
to a customer at a coffee shop in the hospital. I used to know
her in younger days, me hanging onto the median once on Dodge street,
waiting to cross to the mall, while she was driving in her car.
I wasn't organized into words then, trying only to eat, cook
in restaurants not worth mentioning, still trying to bring
together my world, right as it collapsed. I thought something
was there, waiting for my espresso, maybe she'd remember,
but someone else brought my cup. 30 years changed
every world I've lived. There isn't any stable surface to sit across
from any friend I used to know and tell them I love or loved them,
or that time has at least made me less of a body walking in a cold street.

Nobody Ever Listens in America

These words are painted on a wall in America.
This hall in a building exploded from memory,
dangling dangers with a small city in America.

The couches are brown, boring. People sit here,
facing the wall, facing me talking about weather.
Drinking Kool-Aid, squawking about Kool-Aid
drinking it's taste away, no laughing in America.

This wall is decrepit in disrepair, waiting there,
for me to heighten it, it wants more life, less of
it too. I'd give it light, enlighten a corner, fix it,
shed some lights on the eclipse of these uneven
corners it helps contain in this room in America.

The holiday isn't over yet, yearning for lengths
it won't achieve. The people looking at walls in
longing ways. The hallway centered as a monk,
holding their hopes, his breath here in America.

It's just a room, noisy, yelling never understated.
I'm not here for this wall, not to look at my cast
shadow dancing to music in my head of overdue
heroes. My head is more like a prancing boxer's
than a ballerina, both artists. Doom lights its own
fire with gasoline and a match. This is my name,
quiet but less peaceful, banging with time crying,
hoping for fewer tears now while here in America.

Other People's Parties

It used to be easier to go places I didn't want to be   tripping into the doorway
holding onto the wall for balance   there's an indecency in being
strait-laced now   no opportunities to be chaotically dancing in a nightclub
with people that are not aware of their obvious lack of rhythm   their descriptors
being too easy to pinpoint   the woman in the corner just trapped in the music
the man behind her trapped in her corner   wanting more space or just more
to keep going   this is a world where there isn't a stopping place to argue
to get another drink   to get another drink to argue over

it used to be easier to go places I didn't want to be   the possibilities were more robust
thinking of a benefit for leaving my house   I don't like talking about nonsense
nonsense being the primary subject of discussion at a party   people want
to make a difference by convincing you they're important   twirling a glass
it's all wine now or whiskey   nothing of interest   to anyone I once knew holding me
up while I was trying to get into a car   to go to a different party   to examine wildlife
to put a face on and act like some other person   to hack the world for 12 hours
and find out the meaning of life   or the meaning that you've always thought possible
to see   none of this lasts   momentary as lighting a cigarette with a zippo in the wind.

My Wife in Her Own Words

My flowers are a zydeco, moving in the sun, trapping water with their roots,
burning down the sun with their colors. I will sway against the day
that awaits me. Clocks chatter in the background of my office,
wrens angry I'm even there. I want my garden where there is no struggle
or maintenance I've forgotten, no meeting to attend, only what I choose as
silence. Where I understand the necessity for work, to turn the soil, to plant
seeds, to water the lawn. To outrun the dogs as they try escaping through the
backyard gate. I want to outrun, sometimes, myself, my own anxious rubber
ball, juggling nervous paperclips. There is emotion here you cannot see, in the
thoughtful turning of jelly jars in boiling water, dicing peaches, picking sour
gooseberries and currants at midday. You see now how you will miss me, hoping
for a moment to talk about something not so serious. I will say my words,
speaking a language that will not betray silent ways, and you will say more than
you need to about how it is you can no longer paint pictures.

Would You Believe

There is a feeling that changes from excitement to horror,
I don't have a name for it though. It's like I'm looking for
the word for collecting books I never read that I can't think of now.
Maybe it's just a sound. Deftly put upon the ear in the way that makes me
think I see a flock of birds tearing the sky. But there aren't any birds.
Have you ever thought you couldn't believe something was happening?
A tiny exchange in synapses, a spasm truing your mind, making you think
this can't happen.

After I Took Too Much LSD

There is death in my shirt   humbling the onlookers   an assassin with crooked teeth
it's a pattern on a hot line that stifles everything that breathes there is death in your shirt
nobody laughs but some remember   him, spun out, prone in his bedroom \ almost dead
from rat poison   at least for now   shot nerves looking for speed   not a filet mignon or a glass
of wine   it's a hunt to find smallish papers   a paperboy obsessively trying to deliver
the news to himself   despite the frigid temperatures and no coat   a walk in the rose garden
to get there   someone with dirt on their hands might have the proper tools
to work out the immediate problem   the world   looking bent like an alien language
that sound of crackling like hot oil in a cast iron skillet   bent like the back in need of a brace
teleportation as a possible way out   it's just me now   take it   or leave it at the table.

Self Portrait with a Bowl of Apples and My Friend the Painter

Sliding snow prints on canvas, apples dummied against the ground
clumsily. Here I am in foreground, a cigarette and bottle in my bag
looking for a roadmap, which doesn't exist anyway. We can paint
onward and call it, " Falling Over," if that works for you. Hit
the canvas with more paint or your hands to paint, but don't scratch
at the canvas. Of course we can include the falcon hanging
on the tree eating a fresh rat and you picking out thorns from your hands
from hidden decaying leaves. Not everything needs to be present in the
frame,we can ignore details that make us look foolish, the lack of color in
our cheeks can be a rose instead, even smeared on, paint dripping, still wet.

Ars Poetica of the Artist Floating Away

Work is about getting somewhere, the way boats float
even though they're made of steel. Hit your hand on the sides
and you find a solid plain, a pain you didn't know possible.
The hollow sound echoing through it and your body. It's a song
made to test if you can still feel the notes. Lyrics written on legal paper,
you'd send them to someone if you had someone to send them to. I turn
everything to dust, creating the structure, filling in gaps
with wood putty, mounting its creation on a wall
to look closer at what I've done.

The Complications of Living in My Parents House in 1996

The hospital was a better place to find myself then, now it's
overrun by those who have broken too many laws for them to be
tolerated further without adult supervision. I had let my mind
get too far away from painting with long brushes. Flowers
are their own language, just don't send me a can of mixed nuts.
Later, after I quit one job, not intending to get another, I spent time
in a university library reading in earnest about what put me there.
It was too complicated to understand, with Timothy Leary
and Richard Alpert only muddying what was already a picture
with no ground to hold it. My parents didn't know I'd been fired,
but never found it surprising when they did. Anger makes one harden
into a clay pot, so one can carry someone else's problems, or the mind
that dies even though the body still lives. My existence in their home
was clandestine, I didn't want to talk to myself either.
One day my mother told me as I lay, "Just go out and do something."
It didn't occur to me that she meant immediately.

What the Body Will Say When You're Dead

He swallowed pills abilify aristada atenolol benzodiazepine buspar chantix divalproex
sodium lithium paxil warfarin zoloft zyprexa for thoughts that didn't make sense for
fixing a body

He lived smoking a cigarette on the porch in the street in a portrait with ferns a portrait of
placid water black scribbled charcoal marks on paper gutted lungs smoking suicide
smoking as a cure for boredom

He was not unhappy tentative watchful of what was happening women in busses
exploding words on billboards examined voices for context or content assumed what might
be the next shoe thrown against a wall slapping pictures of his life hurtling towards the
carpet

He was reckless with love rarely knowing how math works money in the trashcan pennies
thrown in the street scared spending its conditions loved each thing itself secretly in
psychosis making up lost time trying in monetary terms a painter a cook sometimes
father to unimaginable wordplay to children to forget to ward off hummingbirds leaving the
garden beaming sunflowers each year trying to hold on to one last oakleaf in winter
not even the blackbirds would stay there
perched in the trees

He lived blackwhite rules drawing the hard world a child in grade school sitting at a desk
learning cartoon characters political parties dinosaurs atom bombs mutually assured
destruction tipping points wars over nothing starvation biblical plagues locusts looking for
food in a wheat field rats people scurrying in basements afraid of each other of what it

meant to be alive   without responsibility   learned to break rules of one-sided history books
cracked at the spine then lived history anyway   writing on windows creating mixed-up
suburban graffiti   then quit   returned to the suburbs   tail cut from his body

He knew what he saw   everything always   a declining timeline   even absolutes   the blue
orange sun shining in mornings before descending   a barely working staircase   to make bread
the idea that we're trying to work this dough   enough to make it cohesive to bring together dry
bits of flour   before mixing further   to eat first   by looking   at what's in front of you.

Dark Matter Is a Card Game I've Lost

I will say too much about physics in my life,
sitting down in my living room like Schrödinger's cat
pouring it out so that I can get rid of me. There's something
missing in my embraces, the length of a kiss too short, the way

I've lost my place more obviously than a card game's slanted
rules. The house continues to win, and even though they lose,
patrons keep playing along. I watch myself looking for quarks,
or cards I'll never see in the dealer's hand like dark matter.

I'm only implied in the game, not wanting to interact with
the gravity of the situations that cause me a feeling of wanting,
whether to leave the game or not. Gambling becomes tiring
with all the cards on the table, without chances left. Sometimes

doctors say solar radiation could help me rectify my state, a
bicycle ride on a sunny day or a walk in the park like Einstein,
feverishly considering how not to give the world the way
to destroy itself, to not give away too many secrets.

Different States

There isn't enough time here, not with all the clocks
in the world pointing the same direction. I don't mean
to be repetitive, but I can't help noticing our sins
against each other. Time that lumbers by, waiting
for us to hold hands again and be an old couple growing older.
I know it certainly isn't real.
                                        Dancing a fine line
between walking and walking away, in a state
that doesn't allow for standing in the streets, controlled
by traffic. Denying ourselves the pleasure of consciousness.
The landscape is oily; there's nothing real beyond
the state lines. Even the flowers erupt from ground
that makes you think it would never give life again.

Aftermath and sitting in English Class
—after The Rolling Stones

Sitting in English class feet pressed
against the legs of my chair hoping
for the next 20 minutes to expire, my father
laying in a hospital bed with no exit, no future
of escaping from it. Me thinking I'm separate,
that there's a future return on my time,
that returns don't diminish, that the hospital
is comfortable and not its own death.
That forgetting every memory of getting in a car
with him isn't something I can forget.
He'd put my hand on the stick shift
at stoplights, his hand over top and help me work
the gears, trying to turn me into a driver.
I don't miss it now, but I might later. Time
is always different looking backwards.
There's no way into this without bringing
up music, the time and the rhythm, the meter of
lyrics ringing in my ears, like *the way I talk when I'm spoken to,*
the Stones sang a song from 1966 before he even knew
what the aftermath could really entail. All of us
at some point pay for someone else,
their fuck ups bouldering the path, looking back at you
with pale eyes and skin too white to ignore and no options
to look away at birds, or a child playing with action
figures in a tree. There isn't enough English class
to describe in short sentences the time he has. Since
he no longer wears a watch; his time is perfect. He wouldn't know how
to tell you that he's been indicted for nothing other than being
at the wrong place at the right moment. I don't see him
anymore. He's not there in the usual way, only
substance now, broken body with scarred mobility, the
loops in thoughtless time gone where my mind can't see.

Self Portrait with a Pill Bottle

Pills are a religion to ward off the desire to destroy
someone's religion. A picture of what comes without
them isn't without its terrors: the unoccupied mind
stirring its own cocktail, the failing cardiovascular on a rail, both moving
towards the certainty that without them paranoia would slowly exist,
at a place not unlike a song on repeat you can't help hating,
but cannot stop singing to yourself. They are a prayer.
But I never actually pray, I just swallow pills.

Waiting To Leave

I'm waiting for the day it's less sunny with
more raptors in the trees, waiting for sparrows
sitting in the sunnier side-shadows eating.
I haven't ever told you what I really think of your
sweater sitting in the kitchen—I'm waiting
for that too. I'm waiting for myself
to actually make sense of the lines in this picture, the words
loose in my mouth, teeth knocked free after a punch.
I'm waiting to stop in my chair and sit looking
at you playing at crossword puzzles across
from me. I want you to know I'm here sleeping
next to you with coffee in my hand, not wanting to leave.

Fake Drill

Think of a child's hand, finger pointed drilling
into the sticky meat of your arm. You may not want

this. Think of how they feel wrapped into the stopwatch
on your wrist where there's always ticking, the faint

reminder of trying for an early bedtime or your taxes,
the car parked in the driveway needing an oil change.

You know so much more than they do, pushing numbers,
cleaning the kitchen, taking them with you to see the world

that keeps both of you distracted with shiny toys, digging
the hole further down where you might find them asking

for what you both really want, which is the time of day.

The Dumbest Things I Could Think Of

The narrative I've performed doesn't exist any longer.
There weren't any clowns willing, frightening or not,

to come center stage and perform tricks like juggling
bowling pins in floppy shoes. My life wasn't funny

enough for theatrics, even a dramatic production might
only scratch the surface of what's there. I slammed like

a dead apple thrown against a trashcan, a sophomoric trick,
the waste of momentum or inertia in moving ahead lost

in the action. While worried about death, I turned out bread
pans for a while as penance for everyone I thought I'd scarred.

There's no finding lost things like this, not keys or wallet,
I never seem to know where to look, it's not the time.

I now know the purpose of the unloved objects in my life, with
the dumbest things kept in my pockets, so I don't lose them.

Everybody Loves the Sunshine, in 1995

—after Roy Ayers

I remember listening to the other room as I touched
her arm. She was younger and more willful
and I tried convincing her that my friends were playing
Roy Ayers for me, or us, or anyone but themselves.
Still believing that they loved me, that we were
brothers. What do we do when good intentions are only
a picture in one person's wallet? Are there words left
to say for people gone into their rooms with
nothing to keep them company but the pillow?
She laughed at me and rolled her eyes.

Timeclock

—for V.

I know the timeclock in my memory, hung
next to bottles of cheap whiskey and olives

a stereo that played the popular favorites,
the mirror that everyone could make their face in.

I know it called me the night before, telling
me to get ready early, to be at the café before

the dough was over-proofed, before employees
showed up to throw in a few too many opinions

for me to have to sift through. I know a lot
was only in my mind. Nobody *needs* to work

at 3am. I know gossip was looming around,
it wasn't the rats in kitchen walls, but I worried

about them too, biting my fingers, snarling.
I know I hurt myself for the bread that you ate,
your smile gaunt as each bite passed your lips.

The Last Things to Go in the 1990's

There were so many people wearing
sharkskin suits grey and plastic
left sitting streetside on a side street,

the omnipresent threat of war in places
I didn't want to go, a political nightmare
brewing for oil to start a war. Many agree

I don't need gasoline to start a fire.
To me so much was lost,
like watching all my friends walking

home after the streetlights popped on,
me still on the way home with my bike in tow.
I got lost somewhere before I reached

my house looking at cigarette billboards, me
psychotic and golden, drinking milk and eating
gummi bears. The last things to go were music
that had screaming I couldn't ignore, and birdsong.

The People We Choose to Slow Us Down

I'm a cigarette smoking automaton editing out the parts
of the day nobody can hear without listening as hard as I do.
Death, oncoming traffic, or the noise the cat makes wakes me up,
the thunder from the coffee pot. It's not getting to see you
that makes me want a quiet room to sleep in the architecture
of my day. Some buildings look like they were designed by children,
while others were designed for them. I'm not a child, but barely a man
either, holding onto you to stop spinning off the merry-go-round.
This park has obstacles hidden within, obscuring views from the locals leering,
trying to point to the places we've failed each other. We're meandering
in the trees, finding ourselves lost looking at the ground for a way back.
The trail littered with cigarette butts and old pictures; us
sitting and looking at each other in a summer long since passed.

Self Portrait as a Lazy Man

Bored of card tricks and sleight of hand turning each deck
into a spiral. I'm bored of people playing me, their bugging eyes,
fisherman hats and sunglasses, their use of hallucinogens.
I can't stand the tilted cakebox on the counter,
weighed down by papers and a coffee cup
on the narrow side keeping it there to be looked at.
There isn't anything easy enough to do. Ripping magazines
in search of pretty faces, bearing the wind of this place
reminds of how much struggle this becomes,
and that I'm in a mousetrap, feet dragging behind.

If There's a Place to Keep It All It's Here

If there's a place to keep it all it's here. The blues haunting each record
on the turntable spinning in the direction, you'd think least likely, which is clockwise,
not backwards, at least in this case. This comes from observation. Facing the music
is something else, this told to me as a younger creature worried of consequence erupting
from my father's face marching towards the school with me in tow, for me to see confronting
failure is the only way forward from here. To be told endlessly I had potential, just very little
follow through. I drop the needle on the record now, as the dog walks past and shakes
it loose from the groove, causing a skip. I don't want there to be a last song.

Self Portrait with Rabid Dogs

I tried to pick the best greens for my horrors at seeing
the seething teeth frothing death from aimless mouths,
the reds for bloody reminders in fangs tearing my skin.
The shame is mine for letting them get so out of hand,
I can remember when they liked to play fetch, or sleep
under the couch as I took a nap. I look now and there's
nothing that can call them back, with them melting
at the moment, I am trying to take them home to start over.

Jeff King was born in Omaha, Nebraska in 1974. He developed an early interest in art and spent most of his early years drawing comic book characters and cartoons. He has an avid interest in music, present and past with a record collection spanning everything from Bob Dylan to Kendrick Lamar. In high school, he began writing poetry and continues to learn about language to this day. He is a student at Metropolitan Community College in Omaha, where he began taking writing seriously, and continues to hone his craft. He is a proud father of 2 boys with his wife Jennie, and they still live in Omaha. This is his first book.

www.ingramcontent.com/pod-product-compliance
Lightning Source LLC
LaVergne TN
LVHW090541110826
845146LV00003B/1207

* 9 7 9 8 8 9 9 9 0 4 6 5 3 *